The Road To
Clevedon Pier

This Belongs To

....

....

....

First published 2018 by The Hedgehog Poetry Press

Published in the UK by
The Hedgehog Poetry Press
Coppack House, 5
Churchill Avenue
Clevedon
BS21 6QW

www.hedgehogpress.co.uk

ISBN: 978-1-9996402-0-0

9 8 7 6 5 4 3 2 1

A CIP Catalogue record for this book is available from the British Library.

Contents:

:

The Poems

I WEAR MY KEYS LIKE A GLOVE

Victoria Richards

I wear my keys like a glove
as we walk, hand in
hand, feet crackling
over leaves. Their
metal kiss like armour,
heavy brass my bayonet.
Their supine edges are
knives I'll use to
protect you in this forest
of gold and green, and
a faraway tree that spills
spell-words like Silky and
Moon-Face and the riotous,
crashing Saucepan Man, and
Jo and Bessie and Fanny –
wisha-wisha-wisha.
Here, we are both six.

"Look, a cave." You point
to the darkest trees and I see
an ordinary man, in
ordinary clothes, standing
ordinarily. I see a monster,
a golem waiting in the woods.
and – my heart is a rabbit.
I draw you closer, move
my hand to the side of your
head to remind myself
of your softness.

I force your small legs
faster
faster
faster
until we fly. As we pass him
I cover your ears, lest
you drown in his siren song
of loneliness and need and
wanting, and my keys
are solid
in my hand.

MERCY

Sarah Thomson

In the Sunday sunlight late afternoon
Drug dazed from pain days seeking mercy
Heard that Cornell Campbell reggae tune
Dip my aching head into the icy sea

Out on the streets, into the unknown
Drug dazed from pain days seeking mercy
Up and down steps in the alley alley oh
Dip my aching head into the deep blue sea

Found a path with a bench where I could sit
Drug dazed from pain days seeking mercy
By abandoned buildings and a lamp unlit
Dip my aching head into the icy sea

Passing by the undergrowth where wildlife creeps
Drug dazed from pain days seeking mercy
I made a quick retreat, in fear of sudden leaps
Dip my aching head into the deep blue sea

Back where the blue coats walked by the wall
Drug dazed from pain days seeking mercy
Down the hill wind-blown the Hope & Anchor
Dip my aching head into the icy sea

Heading for the harbour dodging all the cars
Drug dazed from pain days seeking mercy
Past the apartments' balconies and bars
Dip my aching head into the deep blue sea

There on the boardwalk in between the barges
Drug dazed from pain days seeking mercy
There amongst the watercress and frost grey fishies
Dipped my aching head into the icy sea
Dipped my aching head into the deep blue sea

WALKING WITH COLERIDGE IN CLEVEDON

Matt Duggan

On the day the first snow- flakes fell
along a muddied jigsaw shore,
slim boats lined with black blushed tails
smeared grit on brown labyrinth floor.
Path of tobacco and crosses in dead oak
matted with feathers and yellow moss
on waters where lost epiphanies float
above the slewed ringlets in polished frost.

I saw the painting of that man from Ottery
following him along the small palms of frozen sand,
beneath a jacinth coloured moon this wreckage of moonlight –
a circled sinew of bloated white rain.
Vinegar trails in a child's frosty hands
like lines of wax embalmed into cemented snow,
grass verge is a train track rustic and twinned
where a balaclava covered chip-fryer is shivering.

Close to a distant pier with green shining railings
a charred black orchid casted out at sea
vast cloudless sky sailing in dark colours
that can only hear an ocean stopping to breathe.
Car engine coughing among the mists of warming sleet
like fish-hooks that sway in dull twilight;
Winters canvas swallowing pin pricks of zenith light,
that shined on the children playing hopscotch on broken glass.

MOONLIGHT

Sarah J Bryson

Knowing the moon is a solid mass in space, orbiting us
on her regular trajectory, does not stop me seeing
this translucent pearly disc - hanging high and steady
shining bright - as a device for letting light through
into our time, from the other side.

Knowing that your erratic breath will come to a stop
sometime soon, does not deter me from my hope that
in the morning things may be different. I wait, both
wanting time to speed up and for it to slow down
knowing what I wait for may happen before the moon

has completed her lamplight traverse
across the expanse of pinpricked black.

TRUST IN STONES

Annie Maclean

Old texts had outlined the arrival of the aliens:

The explosive rush.
A burning bush.
Haloes of fire.
Ferocious wings.
A brightness
and a cackle of heat.

For thousands of years we were left alone.
Left to wonder what they wanted.
Left to wander round the scratchings
they'd scored across our sparkling stones.

There was a hunger to mine to find more stones.
We wriggled underground
to hunt out fire opals
to set upon a crystal grid.

Green ghost quartz
placed inside sacking
was dragged behind us.
We walked inside darkness.

We stole the nests
of agate eggs which had dragon veins.

From the shores
a collection of ocean jasper,
clear aquamarine
and clouded sea-glass.

On the hillsides
we searched for rainbow amethyst.

We counted out moonstones
not far from the granite.

Two lines were pressed down
made with radiant stones.
Two miles set in a cross
pressed with glistening jewels.

Could we attract their return?

The glinting of lights
would highlight our message.

We learned how to sing
when we sat with the stones.
We named many stars.
We reached out and waited.

FARM

Sally Spedding

They can't see that slack net spread flat on the wall above
their watery tomb in Escouloubre where the river Aude
roars by, flinging spume into summer's overhang. Kissing
its sun-speckled rocks a world away from these doomed
 black trout lurking duped and mute. Not knowing who'll be next
 to fill the café's pretty plates, empty-eyed, mouths agape while
their ribs come clean between swigs of bières blondes and eager
plans of how best to spend the rest of that stunning
afternoon.

THAT'S DEBATABLE

Gaynor Kane

Two words, uttered often
in our house
growing up.

Pierced by the points
of the sunburst clock
and hung from

the walled wire guitar,
like an unfinished
chord, musicless.

Silently soaking
into brown and amber wallpaper;
no discussion from either.

TEA

Hanan Issa

The cup is the first step.
A delicate teacup suggests high teas,
decorated by lace napkins,
and pale gloved fingers
that reach for neatly cut sandwiches,
while the talk slices up an Empire.
A mug of cha to calm the nerves in a crisis
is a match's half-time helping,

that synchronises switches across the country.
But are the builders enjoying their brew
aware of the painful past
contained in its dried leaves?
A politely hidden history
that traded tea for the poppy.
Or that, once in Boston,
pouring tea into water stood

for discarding colonial control.
A sorrow infused over time,
seeping bitterness into boiled water.
Although, when mixed with mint,
jasmine, star anise, or cinnamon,
the taste of history is steeped in the present:
a place we all try to infuse with the taste of us.
Meticulous ceremonies that celebrate friendship:

"Gentle as life, strong as love, bitter as death".
Chai is poured from on high,
spilling along the Silk Road to Tescos.
Merging bitter matcha with sweet shai,
soaking into bara brith raisins overnight.
Cultures and languages permeate life,
weaving through our flow of experience,
iridescent in the chaos.

FROM PARIS TO PITTSBURGH

Chris Hemingway

I'm thinking of moving from Paris to Pittsburgh,
I don't care which ice caps may melt.
I'm building a chain of unMexican restaurants,
from the rust of the bible belt.

I'm dreaming of moving from Paris to Pittsburgh,
no more artist's garrets for me.
I'm dreaming up clickbait for sociopath media
in the land of the guilty and free.

I'm travelling at speed from Paris to Pittsburgh,
in gas-guzzling black & gold jets.
Taking decisions, ice-cold objective,
as amphetamined Vietnam vets.

I'm buying up art from Paris to Pittsburgh,
but Mona Lisa was way too small.
I'm staring at naked impressionist women.
Some paintings to hang on my Wall.

I've just signed up to the Pittsburgh Agreement,
with some guys from Horny Ben's Bar.
We'll limit our gasses by taping our asses
to buckets of over-fracked tar.

See we never moved far from the animal kingdom,
so we'll just have to fry them as well.
It's a mighty long way from Paris to Pittsburgh,
as I drive us by handcart to hell.

REJECTION

WH Davies, Southwark 1899

David Hale

Footsore, a solitary penny in your pocket,
you stump back to the hostel in Churchyard Row.
Without glancing at the sheaf of poems
you've spent days hawking from door to door,
thrust them into the wood-stove and watch
as the ashes of your invention rise
into the city dusk, so consumed with rage
at editors, printers, reviewers the poor souls
you tried to sell verse to, you smack your head
into the chimney-piece again and again,
unable to see how far and wide your work's
being disseminated, your charred rhymes
settling on ledge, gull-wing, roof-tile,
the faint margins of that bleak autumn day.

STONES

P Wooldridge

He seemed so strangely sad to me,
beneath the smeared grey coastal skies.
I ran to help, with infant glee,
beyond my watchful parents' eyes.

Collecting rocks, like he had been,
I pulled them from the tidal sands.
To me, a simply playful scene.
He took them, wordless, from my hands.

Soon bored, I turned, left him alone,
his pockets heavy on the shore.
So innocent, I'd not have known
what I had helped prepare him for.

With years now passed I understand,
what then had made no sense to me,
before returning safe inland
I watched him walk into the sea.

ARTEMIS AT TESCO

Jane Aldous

She didn't look like a hunter but she was.
Middle aged with a black coat and dark lined eyes,
her hands moved fast as she scraped hair from her face,
packed her shopping at the checkout then looked around
with a smile, *I'm ahead of the game*, she said,
handing over a bundle of vouchers. And with that look
I thought, she could swim the Forth or the Acheron,
she could take on anyone.
I last saw her pushing a trolley through the forest
of cars, a bow slung across her chest, arrows in hand,
storming along the high street. Bands of Furies
were bearing down on her, she knew it but she'd
got through worse. That day she was Diana the huntress,
who we looked in the eye and loved because she was like us
and not, *I'm winning*, she said.

BALLOONS.

Mary Gilonne

On the day I nearly left our future,
it was in a wicker basket on ascending currents,
breath tipped with trees, looking down and away.

Morning had seen me dressing, edgy as an insect,
a fleeting reflection of wings multiplied in mirrors,
trying to hold back light, abandon thinning bedroom air.

We'd billowed taut from the downs, tongue-tense, autumn
blight browning the fields and both of us full of louring sky.
Grapes of balloons rose slow, like rainbow bursts towards the sea.

Lifting. I believed leaving could be as simple as this, almost
an easy sigh of slipping land. How to explain that sudden shift
of light, the necessary weight of you, how close I came to falling?

POOIL VAASH*

Ian Stuart

Where the waves have worn
a ragged gash into the cliff.

You can get there at low tide,
feel the sand sink
under your feet, climb rocks
slimed with weed.

Inside, gravel rasps under each step,
sunlight, ambered by the cracked sky,
dribbles down broken strata
to glimmer on the pool beneath.

They find bones here, sometimes – skulls
split like broken eggs
and chipped flints, light as leaves,
yet sharp enough to slice a vein
or scrape a fleece.

The half dark smells of wrack
and sulphur, seep and rot

the slow stink of creation

* Gaelic: Pool of Death

MY BEAUTIFUL BRIDE

Elisabeth Horan

Be my knife-whyfe / be glinty-bad
You are migh lyfe-whife

Hesterprynne me; fuck who u like.
Wear this lyfe-vest; don't drown bad -

Fret in the marriage mud dark and oily as drug trees;
hung fruity in the night -

Lightly does nothing for my libido / teddy,
naughty; knotted limbs / akimbo limbic systems

Razor smart u r & shave me ripe n ready;
we r nothing if not hot n heavy

Yet i carry u lite as pigeon feathers / usher me home
notes from the war zone

Never shot down. O, brave flier; no Crow
Martyrdom suits thee as do my chain-link

Ball bearings resonate 4 u :
a soprano; sticky up for this alto,

Beautiful as Elton; candlelit keys
be my knyfe wyfe / love me lightly;

Dirty Diana, wood-wynd arc de triomphe
the death of my dutiful bride -

Ur smyle like dendritic tentacles
high as this merciful shade-tree.

This is not a funeral for anyone but me.
I know how hard u've tryd /

In this rut; lops of my far-flungs.
Be my knife-whyfe / be glinty-bad.

ON READING DONALD BARTHELME'S *THE SCHOOL*

Andrew Halsig

And it will come someday
all the batteries will have moved
electrons from positive to negative.
Life will stop recording.
Individually it will come much faster.
No one will remember how they laughed
when I called their trainers tennis shoes
because no one will call me anything.
The South Korean's will no longer export
Big Bang and Sistar, but
someone will make new symphonies.
Camera's of tomorrow will see my blue
name it green
and wonder how I saw both life and death
as clouds blew through the sky.
Riding in the ambulance from the
ugly youth Louvre hostel
to comfort the niece of a headsplit aunt
will not have meant anything except to the moment.
George Washington and Trump belong to the same America
and divided countries will be whole again.
The boredom of molecules will drive Earth dwellers to Mars
just to see if it can.
Someone will shout in the name of
Great Spaghetti Monsters
self vindicated as the exploding train
strips sons and daughters from half of London
Shanghai, Dubai, and Cairo.

Hatred will be forgiven or forgotten
and the two will not be different.
Where Shakespeare, either a great man,
A great collection of women,
or some prophet yelling at the sun,
drank spilling wine on Othello—
I stain smoke on a Five Star Notebook
thinking of what to repeat.
None of it will be remembered for its end,
but for the journey and what it was.
Colors will be returned to the ether
Not belonging to a single picture.
And it is not the fundamental datum
That gives fuel to the fire,
But a holy spark meaningless as it is magnificent
and if you could ever explain it all,
it would never burn again.

JUNE

i.m. June Payne (1928-2015)

Ben Banyard

Once, I knocked her plastic Homepride man over,
spilled flour all over the rug during Pipkins.
But that was alright; she hoovered
and put his bowler back on.

She'd show me her bronze boy in the garden
and the sentry holding pokers by the gas fire.

Her angry cats were semi-feral;
they queued at the back door for sweetmeats,
sharpened their claws on the wallpaper.

She laughed like no-one else; there was
scandal in those electric cackles.

Everyone in Monica Road knew Auntie June,
invited her to their weddings, brought her
homemade bhajis, sausage rolls, pakora.

Irish George and Black Country Iris,
Mohammed and Nighat next door, Billy the Lush,
Gwen with the creepy Jesus picture.

She took Small Heath at face value
as it changed through the decades;
that house was her home, whoever lived nearby.

She cared for her mum, then her beloved Len
and when there was no-one left

she lay on the sofa, watched Jeremy Kyle
and drank gin until it was her time.

FRANK

Chrissy Banks

In that very southern university, he and I
were northern aliens, experiments
in academia, mad in love with literature,
first in the family to win a place.

Winter or summer, he shrugged thin arms
into a khaki parka. His hooked nose poked
from a face pale as bleached flour. He kissed me
once, in Anglo-Saxon, rough and slobbery.

Frank couldn't do with borrowed thought.
When he spat words straight from the seam,
hard and black, his tutors' eyes lit up.
He didn't give a toss if they agreed or not.

Analysing Hamlet (*he's fucking fucked*),
evaluating Wordsworth (*that bloke wins first prize
fer turning kids off poetry*), rattling off his own
deranged and genius critique of Hemingway,

he gobbed and scrawled himself a First.
The last I heard, he'd won a scholarship,
soared off to be Frank in New York, while I
wondered what it meant to graduate.

What I'm thinking now, too late, is this:
I could have learned a lot from Frank.

LOCH

Zoë Siobhan Howarth-Lowe

The splash startles me and I see you plunge,
you who disdains even two inches of water, suddenly
head under.
I want to jump in after you, but pause, curious
to see what next. You are moving,
your feet doggy-quick, step beneath the surface.
Are you drowning?
My knees buckle, palms scrabble at the edge
thrust into the murk when bubbles pop against the surface
as you push yourself upwards
your muzzle breaking through the water
a mess of sodden fur.
You point your smug ears towards the wading birds
and scoot off.
Amused I splash in after you.

SPACE AND TIME

Jo Roberts

At the bottom right of my screen
time can be seen blinking way,
space between each seconds digital display
can be filled with four syllables,
strange how an elephant or a tiny flea
can fit easily into this gap between now and then.

UNSPOKEN

Karen Mooney

Old rotten cloths
Hang in that damp
Musty room that
Cannot be aired

Pegged tightly
Many years ago
Heat; condensation
Decaying inside

Windows steamed up
Jammed or locked
Keeping intruders out
And regrets within

SMALL DROWNINGS

Nigel Hutchinson

Spring waves gently
ripple towards the beach,
beech trees beyond the harbour
leave rattled music of leaves on the air,
scent of bonfire ash from the quarry drifting,
a duck ducks and dives,
gulls gull unprepared fish and chip feasters
soaking up the last of a setting sun
along the quay, fag end of the day.

Later wind winds through unlit lanes and alleys
sings through oak and ash like a rosary,
hears secret and scandals in parked cars,
lovers quietly shipwrecked, honeysuckle no longer sweet,
lonely old soak drops his keys, coining phrases makes
molehills out of mountains in the park, boxes shadows.

In shadows by the gate our private detective,
a lifetime of cheap hotels and late-night dives
harbours doubts, who's the mole and who a traitor,
sti fles a sneeze – *bless you a dog walker replies* -
turns up his collar, checks his watch,
stubs his unconscious Woodbine,
turns the corner, corners his quarry,
springs his surprise – will he sink or
will she swim?

Loose-footed drunk, all at sea,
trawls for cigarette butts and coins,
waves his semaphore
arms like flags,
sings "My Way" way off key,
discarded lover walks home alone,
kicks a bunch of keys into the gutter,
night casting a long shadow over tomorrow,
darkness unlocks his tears, waves of regret,
him beached, out of his depth, waving.

THE FIRST WALTZ
رقصة فالس الأولى

#metoo

F H Erba

No supervision three bints on our own.
I was eleven, my cousins just older,
Excited, yet nervous and wanting to prove
I was all grown on the streets of Mansheya.
My nonna told me not to waste all my money.
She meant don't buy ice-cream, I would anyway.

Giggling and smiling, we went on our way.
Enjoying our freedom without chaperone -
no falling, no fighting, nor losing my money.
But we didn't know that those boys who are older,
would call us dark names on the streets of Mansheya.
They bumped us and touched us, but what could we prove?

'Kifaya! Enough!' I tried to reprove.
My big day was ruined, 'Oh, just go away!'
They followed us on through the streets of Mansheya.
I no longer wanted to walk there, alone.
Back to my Nonna's where I felt much bolder,
I turned and I gave them a run for their money.

The wrong note was struck: causing disharmony.
My Nonna fetched Mamty who didn't approve:
my conduct was poor so I had to shoulder
the blame for those boys who could just walk away.
My Nonna's words slapped with a shrill, stinging tone,
'You talked to these boys? On the street? In Mansheya?'

She crossed herself quickly, hail-maryed a prayer;
accused me of laughing whilst spending my money.
My nonna chimed, ' Next time, we'll both chaperone!'
Not only my actions would have to improve:
'Of what were you thinking, child, dressing that way?
You know sleeveless shirts can't be worn when one's older!'

'I've learned my lesson, habibty,' I told her,
'I won't go without you again to Mansheya.'
I looked at my feet before turning away.
The mastica ice-cream, I'd bought with my money
was good for one moment but only to prove
the effects of the day had changed me. I'd grown.

There's only one way, for time costs no money,
I'd wait to be older - dangerous Mansheya -
To prove I could walk you alone, on my own.

Glossary
Bint - Egyptian for girl; in English a derogatory term for a young woman
Nonna - Italian / Egyptian for grandmother
Mamty - Egyptian for my mum
Mansheya - Egyptian for city centre; also the name of Alexandria's centre
Kifaya - Egyptian for enough
Habibty - Egyptian for my love
Mastica - Egyptian for mastic; a popular flavour of ice-cream
رقصة فالس الأولى translates to: dance of the first waltz

DIGNITAS

Nigel Kent

Every day the beauty with the lilac,
latex gloves comes to shower him;
her blue plastic apron barely concealing
contours that no man could ignore.

Before, he might have made a pass
at her but since the stroke he chokes
on words that turn to pebbles in his
mouth and thoughts resist all calls

upstairs to rouse themselves from bed.
So there he stands before her. Naked.
Silent. Pale arms hang flaccidly
at his sides, powerless to prevent

the daily trespass of her hands
that wash away his dignity, bit by bit,
like the dirt swirling and gurgling
down the drain beneath his feet.

SOLSTICE

Melissa Fu

The year's become a candle stub
a taper burnt low, with only a trace
of mornings left to light. I draw close
to the river, walk its banks, ask how
to play out the calendar's coda.

Forgive, says the willow who lost a limb
In April under the weight of too much.
Forgive? The word tastes like chalk and
I wish I hadn't put it in my mouth.
What does it mean? *Only this*:

That when sorrow cloaks the sky and
you lose all appetite for rain and ritual,
visit again the houses you entered first
by sunlight. Go now. On a dry leaf,
on a weak wind, barefoot on cold ground.

That on this, the shortest day coupled
with the longest night, you find solace
in the indifferent rime. Can you accept
numbness when it is the only way
to cross those thresholds?

That however frozen, with no offerings
of clementines and holly, you return
you to yourself, like a lost mitten,
like an orphan's key, like unread ghosts,
waiting to be released. Go now.

REASONS TO FLY

Eileen Carney Hulme

It's not hard being in a room with a dead body
when you do not know what dead means.
That's the good thing about being six, watching
Casper the Friendly Ghost and singing
a *haunting we will go*, captivated by his
efforts to teach an orphaned duck to fly.

Outside January snow builds, inside grief is stuck
in my mother's throat. When she tries to speak
it is a low moaning like my friend Mary's dog
when it wants something. I can't see into that box.
It sits in front of the living room window, in this small
post-war council house, a tall candle either side.

The chair I usually climb on to look out
has been moved and I am alone with the box.
I jump, jump as hard and high as I can.
I remember how easy it was for that duck
to fly and lie on the floor with my toys
wondering who can teach me to fly.

My aunt appears and me and bear
have tea in the kitchen. When the box
is gone I climb onto the chair, through glass
follow cloud shapes, as I search between
and beyond for heaven, where daddy is.
How hard can it be then to fly?

WISH

Hannah-Rose Tristram

Some thoughts colour the
eyes – drops of black ink spreading
through mind's clear waters.

LOOKING INTO THE LITTLE ORCHARD

Diane Jackman

The gate hangs in ruins.
I lay my hand on the wood,
eroded into striations,
as Gramp must have laid
his rough hand on the top rail
a thousand times past.

The Little Orchard, fruit trees
grubbed up long ago,
is choked with thistles
and rank hawkweeds.
Small creatures rustle and scurry
under the sheltering canopy.

I stand out in the kale field.
Here fifty years ago last January
I stood beneath the kale stalks,
their grey-green leaves
dripping ice on to my face,
soaking my pixie hood.

Then I thought this world,
this farm would go on forever;
calving, milking, sowing, harvesting,
on for as long as time. They would
have known, the grown-ups,
not clever, but full of knowledge.

When Gramp laid his hand
on the gate, he knew his action
had a finite number of repetitions,
might have been glad of the fact,
as the cold wind blew off the river
and shook the apple blossom.

MOMENT ON A MARSH

Burnham Overy Staithe, 3rd September 2016

Betty Hasler

In the creek of glass
the up-turned cattle sometimes swing their tails;
and shadows of mud-planted boats squat
among the ripples of a disappearing dabchick.
Tethered buoys tense, about to tug at the tide.

In dreary single file
a laden family trudges to a distant beach invisible
along a path interminable. Through the silence
a sneeze is thrown back from their forerunners.
Their spaniel snuffles hopelessly in the grass.

Inside a veil of green,
a cricket pauses its darting to quiver.
I gaze, as dinosaurs did, at the same sky,
and wait to feel a tide begin to turn,
beneath a benediction of white butterflies.

THE ONLY PUB THAT WILL SERVE US IN STOCKPORT

Isabelle Kenyon

Back then desperate to be seen
on a Saturday night –
grimy pub,
teenagers desperate to fill my lungs
with black soot,
as we head bang
to music we'll hate three years later,
but which currently expresses how alone
we all feel
and how desperate we are
to fit in to a clique.

LEAVING VIENNA

Nicolette Golding

On an old train to Budapest,
the kind with six seats
to a compartment.
I fasten round my neck
my grandmother's necklace
because she was a traveller
in her bones and I am not
and because she married
when almost still a child,
never getting to go anywhere.
Confined.

Small white beads and gold.
Larger cylindrical green ones
interspersed like stations
repeat a pattern. Everything
goes round. I make room
for her beside me. Her voluminous
turquoise kaftan, the large feet
in comfy sandals, our hands
knobbly in our laps.

In her sixties she tore away the straps.
New hair-do, modest bags, one-way
ticket to New York. Ave Marias,
these glass beads
the clasp
a Pater Noster, slipping easy
through my thumb and fingers.

Shlopfwerk, Linzerdorf, Mosonayar Ovar,
decades leaning each
a little on the other: mother
on mother. Never grasping.
Passing on,
passing through.

ADOPTION DAY

Stephanie Hutton

My girl arrives
as new and old as a promise.
Her eyes are empty cupboards
aching for food.
Cocaine-white fingers twitch at her side.
The courtroom of her face questions me,
as calm as the morning after violence.
She clutches her bag like a removed womb.
A smile self-harms her face as
she exhales her old name.

INHALE MY DUST

Gail Ferguson

I knit my own cocoon, soft-padded
proof against the world. Inside
I cannot feel the cold
nor hear the big-beaked bird

that comes for me, stabbing.
Inside my cries are choked,
my limbs hamstrung.
I cannot feel the autumn sun.

I shrink and shrink,
I am become a husk.
Where is my metamorphosis,
the great reveal?

SUNSET IN THE WEST

Liz McDonnell

Talking of our future
for the first time
a thing of clay
to be held
and made in wet fingers
(our hands busy
until now
with the storm
we started years back),
we look through a wide smile
in the earth.
The sea is frozen in silver
a crowd of turbines
sculpt the air noiselessly.

A door swinging to open.
A table set for many.
Our words in different fonts.
All things spoken.

At the end of the lilac sky
a giant peach
finally slips into grey.

Seeing the distance as it is
chastened by its bittersweet metric
we notice a spider
eating the silk
of her web
glands nourished for remake.
Soon after
a new orb
glistens intricately.

GHOSTS AND DARK MATTER

Dido F.

In our peri feral vision
Are dwelling things
We cannot look straight in the eye

It matters that darkness weighs
With irrefutable force
As we are taught knowledge and belief
As twining bedfellows

Your epistemology takes the piss
Denying consciousness of lesser broth
Whist abusing yours with underuse
What else should I not believe in Sir?

Was it just you and me in the primeval soup?
Drawing membrane from our immiscibility
Like a nylon thread to knit a life because
Our union is electric

I hardly think so, Sir
You don't believe in ghosts
Which is why I think we're words short
And never will complete our gap fill

CUT OFF

Georgina Titmus

Salon mirror puddles
lamplight the only client.

Spiteful sullen showers
phone box on the corner.

Door stiff and awkward
piss smell on entry.

Pips demand feeding
conversation starts.

Bled dry of rations
conversation ends.

Door stiff and awkward
waiting figures loom.

Fists in the darkness
knives in the night.

Sprint for salvation
stabbed by the rain.

   Salon mirrors splinter.

FOREIGN CORRESPONDENT

Phil Vernon

The uplands deadened him the more:
where people neatly laid in rows
called louder than in other wars,
by simple geometry; he closed

his ears but year on year the song
joined whispers from elsewhere, to drown
the voice insisting we prolong
our lives. He hears no music now.

Daybreak unrolls – without a sound
the empty landscape is unmasked,
the wind has dropped; and far from sea,

the gulls fly, quiet, above the town.
How wide, the space between what passed
and what he told of tragedy.

HOW DOES FORGIVENESS WORK?

Selma Carvalho

In waves of tenderness
Centrifugal, circling
Reaching outwards
From the edge
Of my
Vulnerable
Recipient
Resilient
Self
Come to me now.

DARK DAUGHTER.

Deborah Gregory

Your brother clasps you
in his arms,
presses his fair head with its curls
against your black-capped skull.

Soon you will be gazing
up at him
with blueberry eyes.

All those blonde cousins
drew me from your scent –
but now I know you
as I know myself.

You are the North, the night sky.

You are the full moon over frozen fields.

You will be morning on the shoreline.

You will be ice in everlasting sun.

And I will hold
my freshly fallen daughter
oh I will hold you
lightly

as if I could
cradle the snow.

ON BEAUTY

Victoria Richards

"Am I beautiful?" she says, and my heart
stiffens in spasmodic rhythm, an extra
                    –
to notice how clear her eyes are, khaki
irises in a black lash frame, or:
sugared almonds laid softly on velvet.
I traverse the kitten fur of her cheek,
count nine – ten – freckles darting across
her nose like rabbits in a sunlit field of my
imagining; that beauty spot, a warren at her
jaw. I stroll luxuriously across her
forehead, brows knitted in helter-skelter
frown, like the slide on the ArcelorMittal Orbit,
178m of meshed red steel.
        – Am I, mummy? Am I beautiful? –
the soft pink of her lips is a sunset so
exquisite there's a kind of horror in it.
Words are poison, they choke me as I
spit them out and it hurts, it hurts
to look at her, it's like staring straight
into
the
sun

Author Biographies:

Annie Maclean is a Gael in exile living on the south coast to hear the sea and feel the sun.

Ben Banyard lives in Portishead, which is just up the coast from Clevedon Pier. His collection *We Are All Lucky* (2018) and pamphlet *Communing* (2016) are both published by Indigo Dreams. He blogs at benbanyard.wordpress.com

Betty Hasler is an aspiring poet who has at last found the time to ponder for weeks over which word to use and where. She lives near Kings Lynn. The poem has appeared in *Jurnets Poetry Voices 2017 an Anthology* published (privately) in 2017 by Graham Jones.

Chris Hemingway is a poet and songwriter from Cheltenham. He has a new pamphlet *Party in the Diaryhouse* published this year (Picaroon Poetry) and has previously self-published two collections on lulu.com. Chris helps with the running of the Cheltenham Poetry Festival, and the Squiffy Gnu Wordpress/ Facebook Poetry Group.

Chrissy Banks lives in Exeter. She is published widely in magazines. Her last collection was *Days of Fire and Flood*. Website www.chrissybankspoetry.com. *Frank* was first published in *The North*.

David Hale: Born in Scotland, David currently lives in a Gloucestershire hamlet. He has two pamphlets out, one from Happenstance, and one from Templar.

Deborah Gregory trained and worked as an actress before winning an Arvon Competition and turning to writing. She has an MA in Creative Writing from Bath Spa University and has had three novels, several poems and some short stories published.

Diane Jackman's poetry has appeared in *Rialto*, *Outposts*, *Happenstance*, small press magazines and many anthologies. She was the winner of the Liverpool Festival, Deddington and Café Writers Norfolk prizes. Starting out as a children's writer with seven books and more than 100 stories published, she now concentrates on poetry. With her late composer husband she wrote several works for choir and the libretto for *Pinocchio* for Kings' Singers/LSO. She has just completed a sequence, *Lessons from the* Orchard and is now working on water poems. *Looking into the Little Orchard* is the poem which won the Deddington Festival poetry competition in 2014, although it was never published or put up on their website.

Dido F lives in Bristol with some of her children and lots of cats. She is an educator and a part time sheep farmer with the commensurate, slightly off-beat, skill set. She has a great love of wild places, edifying company and some fictional bears.

Elisabeth Horan is a poet, mother, student and teacher from Vermont, who enjoys working with horses and spending time with her two young sons. Elisabeth has poems published or forthcoming at *Former Cactus*, *Ginger Collect*, *Rat's Ass Journal* and *Algebra of Owls* among other fine journals. Her first collaborative chapbook is forthcoming in March, 2018, at Moonchild Magazine. She teaches English at River Valley Community College. Follow her @ehoranpoet

Gaynor Kane lives in Belfast. She has been widely published in journals and anthologies in the UK, Ireland and America. The poem is due to be published in a new on-line journal, *Nourish Poetry*.

Georgina Titmus: An ex-sitcom co-writer, Georgina has twice been shortlisted in the Bridport Prize, won LVU2, received an honourable mention in Poetry Pulse 2016 and has poems published in *Luminous Echoes* and *Poems to Keep*. She enjoys staring into space and wild(-ish) swimming.

Isabelle Kenyon is the author of poetry book, *This is not a Spectacle* and the editor of Mind Poetry Anthology, *Please Hear What I'm Not Saying*. Connect with her at www.flyonthewallpoetry.co.uk

Jane Aldous' poems have been commended in the Norman McCaig Centenary Poetry Competition, the Baker Prize, Buzzwords Poetry Competition, the Manchester Writing for Children Prize and she won the Wigtown Poetry Competition in 2012. She's also had poems published in *Northwords Now, Southlight, The Eildon Tree, poetandgeek, New Writing Scotland* and the *DUSK* anthology published by Arachne Press in 2018. She's currently compiling a poetry pamphlet.

Karen Mooney's work has been published by *The Society of Classical Poets* and she has self- published three poetry booklets to support various charities. She has participated in readings and projects for International Women's Day, Poetry Day Ireland, the CS Lewis Festival, community groups and radio.

Liz McDonnell came recently to learning about and writing poetry. It is something she does in stolen moments, busy as she is with her three children and full-time job. She lives in Brighton and knows she's very lucky to occupy the space between the sea and the hills.

Mary Gilonne is a translator, living in France for many years but originally from Devon. She has won the Wenlock Prize, been shortlisted for the Bridport and Bedford Prizes, commended in the Prole, Buzzwords, Elbow Room and Caterpillar prizes. Her work has been published by *Antiphon, Curlew, Smeuse, Snakeskin, Grievous Angel, Ekphrastic Review* and *Emma Press* among others, and in several anthologies.

Melissa Fu is from Los Alamos, New Mexico and lives in Cambridgeshire. Her writing has appeared in publications including *The Lonely Crowd, International Literature Showcase, Bare Fiction*, and *Envoi*. In 2017, she was the regional winner of Words and Women's Prose Competition and one of four Apprentices with the London-based Word Factory.

Nicolette Golding lives in Norwich. She has had poems published in anthologies and on London buses. She's pretty old now but has enjoyed reading and writing poetry since the age of seven.

Nigel Hutchinson digs for potatoes and words. His collection *The Humble Family Interviews* is published by Cinnamon Press.

Nigel Kent lives in Worcestershire. His poetry has appeared in *South* magazine, *Poems to Keep* (Dempsey and Windle), *Anger* (Paper Swans Press), *Lost Things* (Emmas Attic Publishing), *Small Acts of Kindness* (Nottingham Peacebuilders) and *Openings 34* (PSOU).

P Wooldridge: Initially inspired to write following the loss of his father, P Wooldridge has continued to write, in formal styles, on ageing, death, children, and other mundane ponderings that are common for a, disappointingly average, father of two young girls.

Phil Vernon returned to the UK in 2004 after nearly twenty years in various countries in Africa, and in 2012 started writing poems again after a long break. Whereas in the past he wrote in free verse he now mostly adopts formal forms, and finds his words and ideas thus surprise him more often. The poem is in *Poetry Salzburg Review*, issue 32

Sally Spedding: Born and living in Wales, Sally spends part of the year in the Eastern Pyrenees which also inspires her poetry and crime writing. Her work has been widely published and won awards, and this year she will again be judging the International Welsh Poetry Competition.

Sarah J Bryson is a part-time poet, and part-time nurse. She takes a photograph or ten on most days of the week. She runs occasional poetry workshops, and has been involved in a research project taking the arts into residential care. Her poetry has been placed in competitions and published in anthologies, journals and on line.

Sarah Thomson was born and raised in the UK and developed a love of writing from an early age. Having studied English at the University of Exeter, she has had a varied career in publishing, accountancy, and Human Resources and is now a full-time writer. She was recently shortlisted for the Bridport Prize 2017 and was also one of the winners of the Persimmon International Poets Competition 2017.

Selma Carvalho is a London Short Story shortlistee, commended for the Brighton Prize, listed for Exeter Writers Contest and the Berlin Prize among others

Stephanie Hutton is a writer and clinical psychologist in Staffordshire, Uk. *Adoption Day* was previously published in *Calamus Journal*, December 2016.

About The Anthology

'The Road To Clevedon Pier' is our first anthology, our first book at all and to be totally honest I really didn't know how it would turn out. We started by asking ourselves why credible poets would take a chance on a new press nobody had heard of and we didn't know the answer to that - all we could do was hope.

In the end it seems as though we must have seemed vaguely trustworthy (although the attraction of a hedgehog in his red wellies is probably closer to the truth) and the competition and therefore the anthology of the poems and poets longlisted for it, turned out to be something special. There is a real buzz to be had when you are reading submissions and you suddenly find *that* poem and so it was the case with Victoria Richards.

However many other poems I read, Victoria's just drew me back, and I won't apologise for including two of hers, it could have easily been six.

Matt Duggan and Sarah Thomson were 'Highly Commended' as runners-up, and they too produced something that has stayed with me. Such fine margins, and on another day...

But it isn't just about those three, the whole of the longlist managed to reach me in one way or another and I can only hope that you enjoy reading them as much as I have.

To finish the book, I took the liberty of asking Victoria, Sarah and Matt a couple of questions, their responses we reproduce here.

MD
February 2018

Winning Poet: Victoria Richards

Can you tell us what the inspiration for the poem was?

"I was walking home from school through the forest with my daughter, who's five, and became creepingly aware of how small she was - and how little I had on me to protect her. I think women are very aware of their vulnerability - we automatically take precautions, such as holding our keys in clenched fingers if we walk alone at night. We don't even think about it."

When did you write it and where?

"I wrote it on the Tube to work, on the 'notes' section of my iPhone. Most of my poems start out as first drafts in that way. It's one of the only times I have to sit still and to think."

What are you currently writing and what are your forthcoming plans?

"I have been working on both a novel and a poetry collection. I'm in the process of editing both and hope that one day they'll fly out into the world and make successes of themselves."

Highly Commended: Sarah Thomson

Can you tell us what the inspiration for the poem was?

"I'd had a really bad few days with pain in the neck/head but after lots of painkillers began to feel a bit better so went out to Rocotillos, The Triangle, Bristol for a cheeky cappuccino followed by a walk to the harbour. While I was in the café they played Cornell Campbell 'Have some Mercy' - you'll have to read the poem to get the rest of the story..."

When did you write it and where?

"I wrote it over the next few days at home in Bristol. Couldn't get the rhythm right at first but then I realised it needed a reggae beat, like the song that inspired it."

What are you currently writing and what are your forthcoming plans?

"I've got a few poems under development not least of which is a 'cult' poem about a Hedgehog! My ambition is to get a collection published and so I'll definitely be entering the Hedgehog Press collection competition. Not all of the poems will be about Hedgehogs though..."

Highly Commended: Matt Duggan

Can you tell us what the inspiration for the poem was?

"The Inspiration for this poem came from a walk I went on last year when visiting Coleridge Cottage, in Nether Stowey in Somerset, we walked across the Quantocks on a cold and rainy day in September then went for a pub lunch in Clevedon at the Royal Oak. I remember I wrote the first lines of the first stanza in the pub on a beer mat, just imagining Coleridge sat in the corner sipping his ale and then walked around Clevedon along the coastal walkways, and that's where lines from the rest of the poem seemed to just fall into place."

When did you write it and where?

"I wrote some of the poem on a daytrip last year to Clevedon and Somerset, and the rest of the poem was finished when I returned home to Bristol. I always like to jot lines down on a mobile phone and then add them to a notepad when I get home. I eventually finished the final stanza late October last year and after a few edits I'd say it was completed at the end of November."

What are you currently writing and what are your forthcoming plans?

"I'm currently working on my second full collection 'Woodworm', which includes the poem 'Walking with Coleridge in Clevedon' , I also have two new chapbooks available 'One Million Tiny Cuts (Clare Song Birds Publishing House) and 'A Season in Another World' (Thirty West Publishing House) which is due this April 2018.

www.ingramcontent.com/pod-product-compliance
Lightning Source LLC
Chambersburg PA
CBHW031208020426
42333CB00013B/842